The "Reason Why" Books

MAGNETS

Irving and Ruth Adler

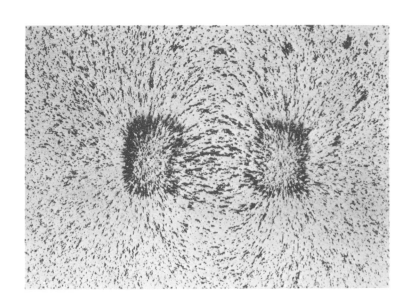

The John Day Company   New York

The "Reason Why" Books
Irving and Ruth Adler

© copyright 1966 by Irving and Ruth Adler

Published by The John Day Company, Inc., 62 West 45th Street, New York, N.Y. 10036, and on the same day in Canada by Longmans Canada Limited, Toronto.

Library of Congress Catalogue Card Number: 66-15091.

Manufactured in the United States of America

Contents

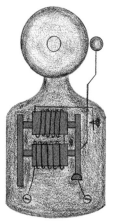

Magnets

A toy magnet can pick up small pieces of iron.

There are many man-made magnets that are not toys. Some are parts of things that we use every day. The needle in a scouting compass is a magnet. There is a magnet in an electric bell and in a telephone receiver. There are magnets in electric motors. There are also magnets in radio sets and in a television picture tube.

Some magnets are not made by man, but are found in nature. In fact, the first magnet ever used is a kind of stone. The ancient Greeks found many stones of this kind in the district of Magnesia (mag-

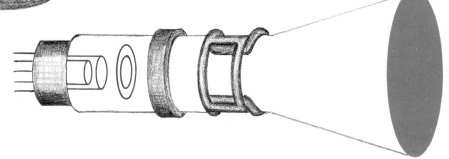

NEE-shuh). For this reason the stone is now called *magnetite* (MAG-nuh-tite — stone found in Magnesia), and anything that behaves like it is called a *magnet*.

Actually there are small and large magnets everywhere in nature. The smallest magnets we know are found inside the atoms of which all things are made. The planet Earth, on which we live, is a very large magnet. The sun is also a magnet. The galaxy, a family of over one hundred billion stars, one of which is the sun, is a magnet too.

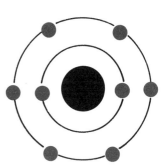

This book tells you about all these magnets that are in the atoms, on the earth, and among the stars.

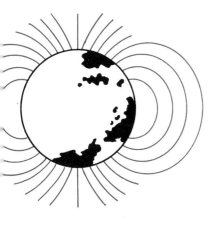

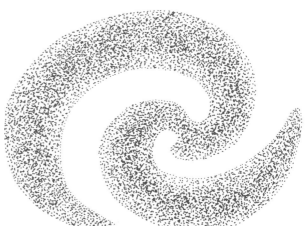

Strongly and Weakly Magnetic Things

There are some things that a magnet will cling to. If they are small enough, it can pick them up. Things that a magnet can cling to or pick up are said to be *strongly magnetic*.

There are other things that a magnet will neither cling to nor pick up. These things are said to be *weakly magnetic*.

If you have a toy magnet, you can see for yourself which things are strongly magnetic and which are weakly magnetic.

A magnet will pick up a paper clip made of iron. It will cling to a pot cover made of stainless steel. So iron and steel are strongly magnetic. Other strongly magnetic materials are nickel and cobalt.

A magnet will not pick up or cling to a wooden toothpick, a brass curtain ring, a copper penny, a silver dime, a glass tumbler, or an aluminum pot. So wood, brass, copper, silver, glass and aluminum are all weakly magnetic.

Making a Magnet

Anything that is strongly magnetic can be made into a magnet. For example, an ordinary paper clip made of iron is not a magnet. It will not pick up another clip. But if a magnet is held very near the clip, then the clip will pick up another clip. This shows that a piece of iron that

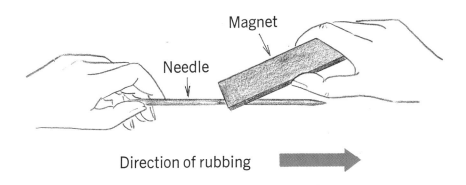

Magnet

Needle

Direction of rubbing

To magnetize a needle rub it many times in only one direction with one end of a magnet.

is brought near a magnet becomes a magnet itself. We say that the iron near the magnet has been *magnetized,* and that it has gained *magnetism.* If the iron is then moved far away from the magnet, it loses its magnetism. The harder the iron is, the more slowly it loses its magnetism. If a needle made of steel, which is a hard iron, is magnetized in this way, it holds its magnetism for a long time. A magnet that holds its magnetism for a long time is called a *permanent magnet.*

A better way to magnetize a needle is to rub it many times with a magnet. Rub it with only one end of a magnet. Be sure to rub it in only one direction, from one end of the needle to the other end.

Another way of making a magnet is described on page 17.

A horseshoe magnet   **A bar magnet**

The Poles of a Magnet

A magnet that is straight is called a *bar magnet*. A magnet that is bent in the shape of the letter U is called a *horseshoe magnet*.

If a bar magnet or a horseshoe magnet is dipped into a pile of small iron nails, it will pick up some of them. More of the nails will cling to the two ends of the magnet than to any other part of it. This shows that the magnetism of a magnet is strongest at its two ends. The two ends of a magnet, where its magnetism is strongest, are called its *poles*.

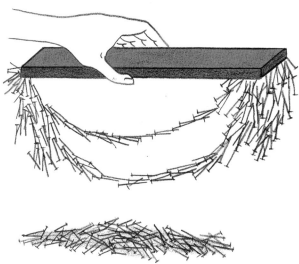

The magnetism of a magnet is strongest at its two ends. The ends are called the poles.

8

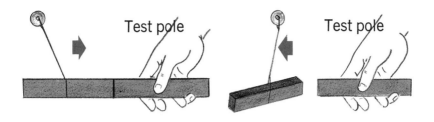

A test pole pulls or attracts some poles and pushes or repels others.

If a pole of one magnet is brought near a pole of another magnet, one of two things will happen. Either the poles will pull toward each other, or they will push apart. In the first case we say that they *attract* each other. In the second case we say that they *repel* each other.

Suppose we choose one magnet to use as a test magnet, and choose one of its poles to use as a test pole. Then we can divide the poles of all other magnets into two families. One family consists of all the poles that are attracted by the test pole. The other family consists of all the poles that are repelled by the test pole. If two poles belong to the same family we say that they are *like* poles. If they belong to different families we say that they are *opposite* poles.

If we bring each of the two poles of a magnet near the test pole, we find that the test pole attracts one of them and repels the other one. This shows that the *two poles on a magnet are opposite poles.*

If we bring two like poles or two opposite poles near each other, we find that *two like poles repel each other*, and *two opposite poles attract each other*.

To name the poles of a magnet, we use the earth as a test magnet. The earth is a great magnet, with one pole in the Arctic Ocean, near the eastern shore of Canada, and the other pole on the opposite side of the earth. If a bar magnet is supported so that it can turn freely, and no other magnets are near it, the magnetism of the earth makes it turn until it points north and south. The pole of the magnet that points north is called a *north-seeking pole* or a *north pole.* The pole that points south is called a *south-seeking pole* or a *south pole.* A magnetic *compass* is a magnet used in this way to point out north and south.

Be careful not to mix up the magnetic poles of the earth with the North and South Poles of geography. The magnetic poles of the earth are the places on its surface where its magnetism is strongest. The North and South Poles of geography are the ends of the earth's axis around which the earth spins.

The north-seeking pole points to the north.

The south-seeking pole points to the south.

N- - - -

- - - - -S

Magnetic Fields

A magnetic pole pulls or attracts poles of the same kind, and pushes or repels poles of the opposite kind. A pull or a push is called a *force*. The strength of the force with which one pole pushes or pulls another depends on the distance between them. The farther apart they are, the weaker the force is. The unit of force used for measuring pushes and pulls is called a *dyne*. The unit of length used for measuring distances is called a *centimeter*.

Two poles are said to be of equal strength if they exert the same force at the same distance on any other pole. Two poles of equal strength are called *unit poles* if the force they exert on each other is one dyne when the distance between them is one centimeter. The strength of any pole is the number of unit poles of the same kind that together have the same strength as that pole.

The magnetism of a magnet reaches out into the space around it to push or pull the poles of other magnets. Because of this fact we say that a magnet is surrounded by a *magnetic field*. To measure the strength of a magnetic field at any point, we use a unit north pole as a test magnet. The force with which a magnet pushes a unit north pole that is held at some point in the space around the magnet is called the *strength of the magnetic field* at that point. Magnetic field strength is measured in units called *gauss* (pronounced gouse). The earth's magnetic field, where it is strongest, has a strength of about three-fourths of one gauss. The strength of the magnetic field between the poles of a toy horseshoe magnet is a few hundred gauss.

To picture the magnetic field around a magnet we draw a series of lines joining the north and south poles of the magnet. The lines are more crowded where the field strength is stronger, and less crowded where the field strength is weaker. These lines are called *lines of force*. A magnetic compass placed at a point in a magnetic field would come to rest along a line of force. The direction in which the north end of the compass then points is called the direction of the magnetic field at that point.

If a sheet of paper is placed over a magnet, and iron filings are sprinkled over the paper, each filing behaves like a small magnetic compass, and lines up on a line of force. In this way the filings form a picture of the magnetic field around the magnet.

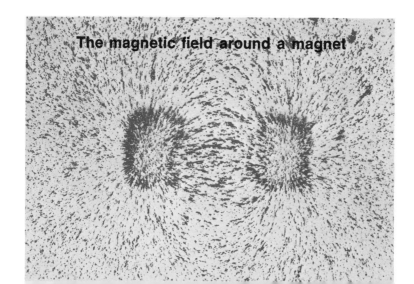

The magnetic field around a magnet

Combined Magnets

Two small bar magnets can be put together to make a single bar. This can be done in several ways.

If the north poles of both magnets point in the same direction, we say the magnets are *parallel*. Parallel magnets can be pushed together side by side to make a wider magnet. The two poles held together at each end are of the same kind. They work together when they push or pull other poles. So together they behave like a single pole of double strength. Because of this, the wider magnet is stronger than each of the narrow magnets of which it is made.

Parallel magnets can be put end to end to make a longer magnet. The poles of this longer magnet are the same strength as the poles of the shorter magnets of which it is made.

If the north poles of both magnets point in opposite directions, we say the magnets are *antiparallel*. If anti-

Parallel magnets end to end make a longer magnet.

Parallel magnets side by side make a stronger magnet.

N		S
S		N

Antiparallel magnets side by side make a weak magnet.

parallel magnets are put side by side, each pole is near a pole of the opposite kind, so the magnets cling to each other to form a wider bar. The two poles that are together at each end of the bar are of opposite kinds. They work against each other. When one of these poles pushes a pole of another magnet, the other pulls it. The result is the same as if there were hardly any push or pull at all. So when two antiparallel magnets are placed side by side, the wider bar they form behaves as if it were a very weak magnet. In an antiparallel pair of magnets, each magnet wipes out most of the magnetism of the other.

Suppose many small bar magnets are put into a box and are shaken up so that the magnets are jumbled, pointing in many different directions. For each magnet pointing in one direction there will probably be one nearby that points in the opposite direction. Together they form an antiparallel pair, in which each magnet wipes out most of the magnetism of the other. As a result most of the magnetism of practically all the magnets in the box is wiped out. For this reason, the boxful of jumbled magnets behaves as if it were a very weak magnet.

The result is quite different if the bar magnets are

Jumbled magnets add up to a weak magnet.

stacked neatly in the box so that they are all parallel. Then the magnets that are side by side add their strengths, and the boxful of stacked magnets behaves like a very strong magnet.

If a bar magnet is cut either lengthwise or crosswise many times, the pieces turn out to be parallel magnets. This suggests that the bar magnet is made of many small magnets stacked side by side and end to end, like the stacked magnets in the box. We shall see later what these small magnets are.

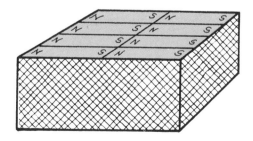

Neatly stacked magnets add up to a strong magnet.

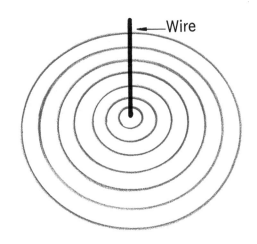

The red circles stand for the magnetic field around an electric current flowing through a straight wire.

Magnets Made by Electric Currents

Magnetism is related to electricity in two ways. Electric currents can be used to make magnets, and magnetism can be used to make electric currents.

An electric current is always surrounded by a magnetic field. If the current flows through a straight wire, the magnetic lines of force are circles around the wire.

A wire wound into a coil, like a coiled spring, is called a *solenoid* (SO-luh-noyd). If an electric current flows

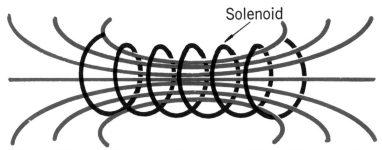

The red lines stand for the magnetic field around an electric current flowing through a solenoid.

16

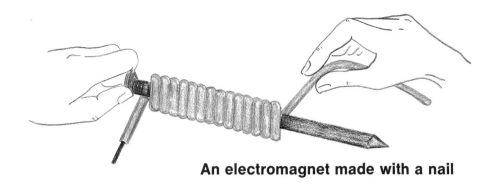

An electromagnet made with a nail

through a solenoid, the solenoid becomes a bar magnet, with a north pole at one end, and a south pole at the other end. If a rod of soft iron is inside the solenoid while the current flows, the magnetism of the solenoid makes a magnet of the iron. Then the magnetism of the iron is added to the magnetism of the solenoid to make it a stronger magnet. A magnet made in this way with the help of an electric current is called an *electromagnet.* There are electromagnets that are U-shaped and with other shapes as well.

To make an electromagnet, wind No. 18 insulated copper wire around a large iron nail. Then connect the ends of the wire to the terminals of a battery.

In a telegraph receiver, pulses of current through the coil of an electromagnet make its magnetism go on and off. Then the magnet pulls and lets go an iron arm that clicks out the message.

In an electric motor there are two electromagnets. One that stands still pushes the other and makes it turn.*

* For a description of the electromagnets in a bell, a telephone receiver and a motor, see *Electricity in Your Life*, by Irving Adler, The John Day Company, New York.

17

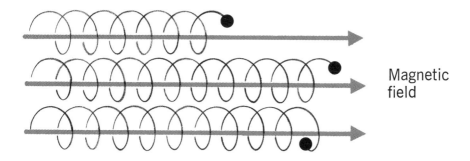

A moving charge in a magnetic field spirals around a line of force.

An Electric Charge in a Magnetic Field

There are some bodies that carry an electric *charge.* Electric charges push or pull on each other just as magnetic poles do. If a moving electric charge enters a magnetic field, the field makes the charge turn aside from its path. This happens because a moving electric charge is like an electric current. Like an electric current, it is surrounded by a magnetic field. The magnetic field that the charge has entered pushes against the magnetic field that surrounds the charge, the way two magnets push against each other. This push makes the moving charge turn aside.

After the moving charge has turned aside, it has a new path. The magnetic field makes it turn aside from this path, too. For this reason, a moving charge in a magnetic field keeps veering as it moves forward. As a result it follows a spiral (SPY-ruhl) path, twisted like a corkscrew around a line of force in the magnetic field. Because of this, a magnetic field is like a trap for moving electrical charges. It captures them and guides them along its lines of force.

The sun throws out sprays of charged particles all the time. They stream away from the sun in all directions. Those that pass near the earth enter the earth's magnetic field. The field then captures them and guides them along its lines of force toward the earth's magnetic poles. When large numbers of particles enter the air near the poles, they make the air glow with bright flashes of colored light. In the north these flashes of light are known as the *northern lights.*

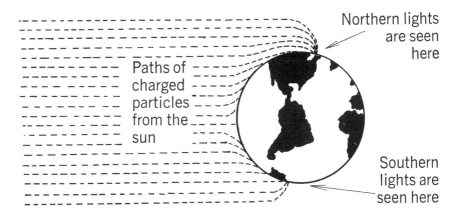

Charged particles from the sun, captured by the earth's magnetic field, make the air glow with the northern and southern lights.

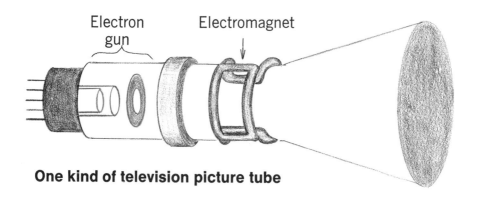

One kind of television picture tube

There are many instruments in which we use a magnetic field to guide a stream of charged particles.

In a television picture tube there is an *electron gun* that fires out a stream of *electrons*. Each electron has an electric charge. In some tubes there is an electromagnet that has a rapidly changing magnetic field. This field guides the stream of electrons so that it sweeps across the face of the tube in lines one under the other, like the lines of words on this page. When the electrons strike the face of the tube, they make it glow to produce the television picture.

The *synchrotron* (SINK-ruh-tron) is an instrument used in atom-smashing experiments. It has a large circular track in which charged particles are pushed by electrical forces. The magnetic field of a great magnet built around the track guides the particles so that they move around the track. When the particles have a high speed they are allowed to hit the atoms that are to be smashed.

The mass *spectrograph* is an instrument for separating charged particles by their weight. A stream of particles with different weights is sprayed into a magnetic field. The field makes each particle veer. But it makes the light-weight particles veer more than the heavyweight particles, in the same way that a wind blowing across their path would make a Ping-Pong ball veer more than a golf ball.

There are some experiments that are being made with hot gases of charged particles. The gases are so hot that they would melt the walls of any container. But the walls do not melt because there is a magnetic field in the container. The field traps the particles and keeps them away from the walls. A magnetic field used in this way is called a *magnetic bottle*.

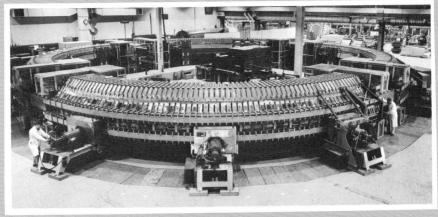

A synchrotron

Electric Currents Made by Magnets

Magnets can be used to make an electric current. If a closed loop of wire is moved through a magnetic field, a current begins to flow through the wire. The same thing happens if the magnetic field around the wire is made stronger or weaker or if its direction is changed. In a *generator* that produces electric power, there are many loops of wire wound around a *rotor*. A rotor is something that can turn like a wheel. The electric power is produced by making the rotor turn between the poles of a large magnet.

If an electric current is already flowing, it is surrounded by its own magnetic field. If an outside magnetic field is added to it by bringing a magnet near it, the added field makes the current either speed up or slow down. The change in the current changes the magnetic field that belongs to the current. This change always opposes the outside magnetic field so that it is made weaker. This fact is known as *Lenz's law.*

Rotor

Magnet

An automobile electric generator

Electromagnetic Waves

An electric charge is surrounded by a field of force that can push or pull other electric charges. This field is called an *electrostatic field*. If the charge is moving, so that there is an electric current, it is also surrounded by a magnetic field. If the current changes its speed or direction, a change is made in both of these fields. The change is like the splash made in the surface of a pond when a stone is thrown into it. Just as the splash makes a water wave travel over the surface of the pond, the change in the current makes a wave travel through the electrostatic and magnetic fields. This wave is called an *electromagnetic* wave. It travels with the speed of light.

Radio waves are examples of electromagnetic waves.

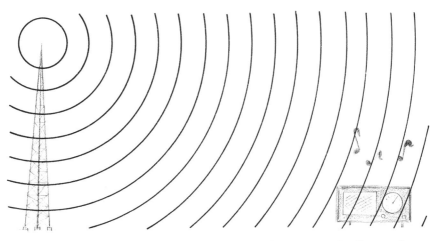

A radio station sends electromagnetic waves to the antenna of your radio.

23

At a radio station, a transmitter makes an electric current that moves back and forth in the antenna. The changing current makes the radio waves that travel from the antenna of the radio station to the antenna of your radio receiver.

Electromagnetic waves are also sent out by charged particles that spiral around a magnetic line of force. If the particles have a speed that is almost the speed of light, the waves are called *synchrotron radiation*, because they are like the waves sent out by particles racing around the track in a synchrotron.

Light, heat rays, ultraviolet rays, and X rays are other examples of electromagnetic waves.

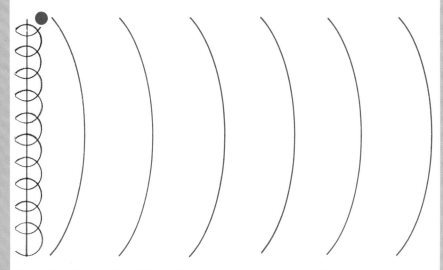

A spiraling electric charge sends out electromagnetic waves.

Magnetism in the Atom

All things are made of tiny units called *molecules* (MOLL-uh-kyouls). Each molecule is made up of smaller units called *atoms.*[*] Scientists have formed a picture of the atom that explains how atoms behave. The picture of the atom shows that every atom is a small magnet. Here is the reason why:

Every atom is made of a small lump called a *nucleus* (NEW-klee-uhs) surrounded by electrons. The nucleus has an electrical charge of the kind called *positive*. Each electron has an electrical charge of the kind called *negative*.

[*] See *Atoms and Molecules* by the same authors, The John Day Company, New York, 1966.

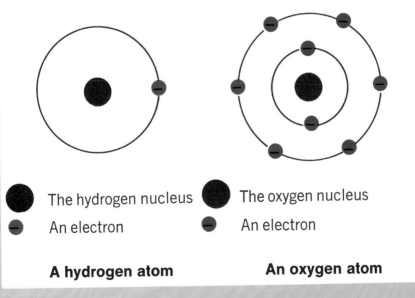

The hydrogen nucleus   The oxygen nucleus

An electron   An electron

A hydrogen atom   **An oxygen atom**

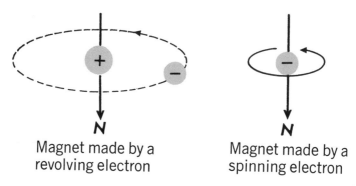

Magnet made by a
revolving electron

Magnet made by a
spinning electron

Two kinds of little magnets inside an atom

The electrons in an atom are moving in two different ways: 1) The electrons revolve in orbits around the nucleus the way the earth revolves around the sun; 2) each electron spins around an axis like a top.

An electron moving around an orbit or spinning like a top is like an electric current flowing through a solenoid. But an electric current flowing through a solenoid makes it a magnet. So there are two kinds of little magnets inside every atom: 1) the magnet made by the motion of the electrons in orbits around the nucleus; 2) the magnet produced by the spin of each electron.

There is also a third little magnet in the atom, made by the spinning of the nucleus. This magnet plays no part in the things we are talking about, so we shall pay no more attention to it.

The small magnets in the atom combine to make the atom itself a magnet.

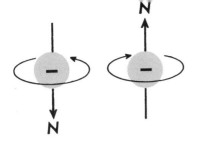 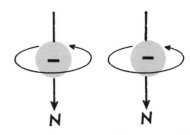

Two electron-spin magnets that are antiparallel **Two electron-spin magnets that are parallel**

The little magnets made by two spinning electrons can combine in only two ways. The electrons may spin in the same direction. Then the little magnets are parallel and combine to make a stronger magnet. Or the electrons may spin in opposite directions. Then the little magnets are antiparallel and wipe out each other's magnetism. In this case we say the electrons are *paired*.

In some molecules, all the electrons are arranged in pairs that spin in opposite directions. The magnetism caused by their spins is all wiped out. So the only magnetism in such molecules is the magnetism of the motion of the electrons in their orbits.

In other molecules, nearly all the electrons are in pairs that spin in opposite directions. But the rest of the electrons spin in only one direction and combine to make a stronger magnet. In these molecules, the magnetism is made of two parts. One part is the magnetism of the motion of the electrons in their orbits. The other part is the magnetism of the spinning of those electrons that are not paired.

Two Kinds of Magnetic Things

When something is put into a magnetic field it changes the strength of the magnetic field. If it makes the field weaker we say that the thing is *diamagnetic* (DIE-uh-magnetic). If it makes the field stronger, we say that the thing is *paramagnetic* (PAA-ruh-magnetic). Glass, copper, silver, quartz and water are diamagnetic. Aluminum, oxygen, iron, cobalt and nickel are paramagnetic.

Paramagnetic things are attracted by a magnet. Diamagnetic things are repelled by a magnet. When a rod is hung between the poles of a horseshoe magnet, if it is paramagnetic, it turns until it lies along a line of force. If it is diamagnetic, it turns until it lies across the lines of force.

The theory of the atom explains why some things are diamagnetic while other things are paramagnetic.

If all the electrons in the molecules of a thing are paired, its magnetism comes only from the motion of its electrons in their orbits. When such a thing is put into a magnetic field, the field changes the motion of the electrons. According to Lenz's law, the change opposes the magnetic field and makes it weaker. So such things are diamagnetic.

If some of the electrons in the molecules of a thing are not paired, its magnetism is made of two parts, the magnetism of the motion of the electrons in their orbits, and the magnetism of the spins of the electrons that are not paired. When such a thing is put into a magnetic field, two things happen. The motion of the electrons in their orbits is changed, and this makes the magnetic field weaker. But, at the same time, the little magnets of the unpaired spinning electrons line up along the lines of force of the field. They add their magnetism to the field and make it stronger. The strengthening of the field is greater than the weakening of the field. The final result is that the field is made stronger, so such things are paramagnetic.

If a paramagnetic rod is hung between the poles of a horseshoe magnet, the rod turns until it lies along the lines of force.

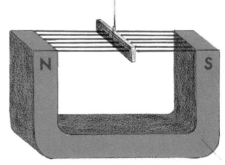

If a diamagnetic rod is hung between the poles of a horseshoe magnet, the rod turns until it lies across the lines of force.

The Magnetism of Iron

All diamagnetic things are weakly magnetic. Most paramagnetic things are also weakly magnetic. But there are some paramagnetic things that are strongly magnetic, as iron is. We say that they are *ferromagnetic*, which means "magnetic like iron."

Iron is strongly magnetic for two reasons. First, each iron atom is a strong magnet. Secondly, iron atoms that are near each other line up like stacked magnets to make a very strong magnet.

An iron atom has 26 electrons revolving around its nucleus. The electrons are arranged in layers called *shells*. Twenty-two of the electrons are grouped in pairs that spin in opposite directions. The other four electrons are not paired. They spin in one direction only, so that the magnets caused by their spins combine to make a stronger magnet. The strength of the magnetism of one spinning electron is called a *Bohr magneton* (BAWR MAG-nuh-tahn). The magnetism of an iron atom comes mostly from the four spinning electrons that are not paired. So its strength is about four Bohr magnetons.

An iron bar is made up of small parts called *domains* (doe-MANES). As many as one thousand domains side by side may be needed to fill out an inch. Each domain has over ten thousand million million atoms in it. Each atom is a small magnet. The atoms in a domain tug at each

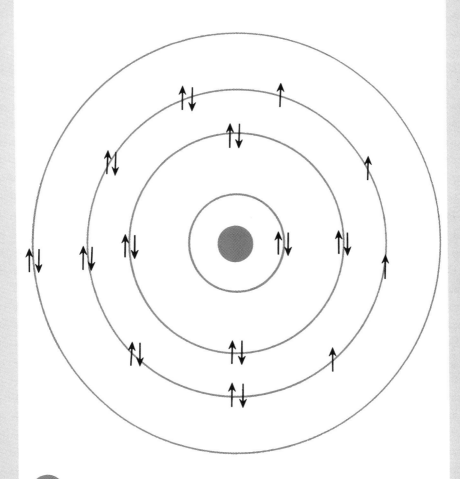

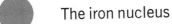 The iron nucleus

↑ or ↓   The magnet of spinning electron. The arrow-head stands for the north pole of the magnet.

Diagram of an iron atom

other with a force called the *exchange force*. This force makes the small atomic magnets in the domain line up side by side and end to end like stacked parallel magnets in a box. The strength of the small magnets is combined to make the domain a bar magnet.

In an iron bar that has not been magnetized, each domain is a bar magnet. But the domain bar magnets point in many different directions, and they are arranged in antiparallel pairs. As a result the magnetisms of the domains wipe each other out, and the iron bar is not a magnet. But if the iron bar is placed in a magnetic field, the domain magnets that are almost in line with lines of force of the field grow while the others shrink. Then the domains are almost like parallel magnets stacked side by side and end to end in a box, and they combine to make the whole iron bar a magnet.

The magnetism in the domains of an iron bar can be destroyed by heat. Heat makes the atoms in the bar wiggle around.* So while the exchange force works to line up the atomic magnets in a domain, the heat in the bar pushes them out of line. The hotter the iron is, the more of the atoms are pushed out of line. At a temperature of 1420 degrees Fahrenheit, the atomic magnets in a domain are completely mixed up, like magnets shaken in a box. Then the iron is no longer strongly magnetic.

* See *Heat* by the same authors, The John Day Company, New York, 1964.

An iron bar is made up of small parts called domains. The lines are the boundaries between the domains.

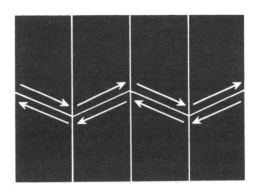

Domains in unmagnetized iron. Each arrow represents a domain magnet.

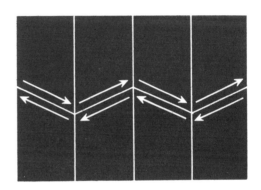

Magnetic field →

A magnetic field makes the domains that are nearly parallel to it grow.

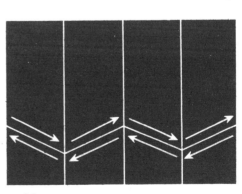

Other Magnetic Materials

The metals cobalt, nickel and gadolinium are strongly magnetic, like iron. Other strongly magnetic materials can be made by mixing one or more of these metals with some other metals and melting them together. A mixture made by melting together different metals is called an alloy (AA-loy). Very strong permanent magnets are made from an alloy called *alnico*. Alnico is a mixture of aluminum, nickel, cobalt, copper and iron.

When a metal is combined with oxygen, the compound is called an *oxide*. Magnetite, the first strongly magnetic material ever used, is an oxide of iron.

Some new strongly magnetic materials called *ferrites*

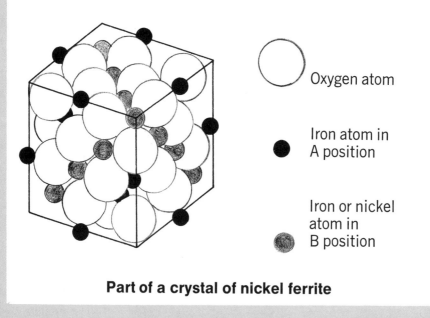

Oxygen atom

Iron atom in
A position

Iron or nickel
atom in
B position

Part of a crystal of nickel ferrite

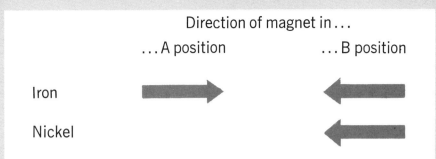

Direction of magnet in...

...A position   ...B position

Iron

Nickel

Atomic magnets in a molecule of nickel ferrite

are now being made by combining iron oxides with oxides of other metals. For example, nickel ferrite is a compound in which each molecule has one nickel atom, two iron atoms and four oxygen atoms. In a crystal of this compound, the oxygen atoms are like a pile of balls. The atoms of the metals iron and nickel are in the spaces between the balls. In some spaces a metal atom has four closest metal atom neighbors. These spaces are called *A positions*. In other spaces, a metal atom has six closest metal atom neighbors. These spaces are called *B positions*. As magnets, all atoms in the A position point in one direction, and all atoms in the B position point in the opposite direction. Half of the iron atoms are in the A position and half are in the B position. So their little atomic magnets wipe out each other's magnetism. All of the nickel atoms are in the B position. So their little atomic magnets are parallel, and combine like stacked magnets in a box, to make the crystal a strong magnet.

Very Strong Magnetic Fields

The magnetic field near a piece of magnetite has a strength of only a few hundred gauss. Near a pole of a permanent magnet made of an alloy like alnico, the strength of the magnetic field is at most ten thousand gauss. Electromagnets made of coils wound around iron have produced magnetic fields as strong as thirty thousand gauss. They could produce stronger fields if they were made larger with more iron, but then they would be too big and heavy to be useful. For this reason scientists have built some new kinds of electromagnets that can make strong magnetic fields without using a lot of iron.

To build these new magnets they had to solve the problem of getting rid of the heat produced by an electric current. When an electric current flows through a wire, the wire tries to hold the current back. This holding back action is called *electrical resistance*. When a current flows, the resistance of the wire changes some of the electrical energy into heat. If this heat were allowed to build up in a very strong magnet, it would *vaporize* (VAY-puh-rise) the coil, or turn it into a gas.

Another problem they had to solve arises from the pressure inside a magnet. A magnetic field pushes against an electric current. If the current is steady and the magnetic field is hundreds of thousands of gauss, the push is strong enough to break the copper coil.

One way of solving these two problems is to use short pulses of current instead of a steady current in the coil. During each pulse there is not enough time for the coil to vaporize or break. Meanwhile streams of water flowing through the magnet carry away the heat formed by each pulse, so that the heat does not build up. At the National Magnet Laboratory in Cambridge, Massachusetts, there

250,000-gauss magnet of the National Magnet Laboratory

Part of a coil of the 250,000-gauss magnet. Cooling water is pumped through the holes in the plate.

is a pulsed magnet that produces a magnetic field of 250,000 gauss. It is made of three copper coils, one inside the other. Each coil is a copper plate wound in a spiral. There are holes in the plates through which water is pumped to remove the heat. The magnet is three feet wide, with a two-inch hole in the middle, and it weighs three tons. It uses 16 million watts of electrical power. Water flows through it at the rate of two thousand gallons a minute.

Another way of solving the heat problem is to make the coil of a material that has no electrical resistance. Then a current through such a coil produces no heat. In 1911 it was found that certain metals lose their resistance when they are made so cold that there is almost no heat in them. When a metal has no resistance it is called a *superconductor*. When the magnetic field near a superconducting metal is above a certain strength known as the *critical field*, the resistance of the metal is restored, and it stops being a superconductor. So a very strong magnet can be made of a superconductor only if it has a high critical field. New metal alloys have been made that do have a high critical field. Among these are niobium-tin and vanadium-gallium. Now magnets made of superconductors can produce fields as high as 100,000 gauss, and may be able to reach 170,000 gauss.

A superconducting magnet

The Magnetism of the Earth

Why is the earth a magnet?

Scientists now think that the earth is a magnet for the same reason that an atom is a magnet: because of electric currents in it.

The earth's magnetic field is made up of two parts. One part is fairly steady for as long as a year. This part is called the *main field*. The other part changes during the day and from day to day. This part is called the *transient* (TRAN-shent) field. The main field is probably produced by electric currents inside the earth. The transient field is caused by electric currents high up in the air.[*]

The earth is a ball that is about eight thousand miles wide. By studying the way earthquake waves travel through it, scientists have found that it is made of three parts. At the center of the earth is a ball called the *core* that is about half as wide as the earth. The inner half of the core, and perhaps even all of it, is mostly iron and nickel. The outer half of the core, and perhaps even all of it, is a liquid. Nearly all the rest of the earth is made of solid rock, and is called the *mantle*. The mantle is surrounded by a thin layer called the *crust*.[**]

[*] See *Seeing the Earth from Space*, by Irving Adler, The John Day Company, New York, 1961.

[**] See *The Earth's Crust*, by the same authors, The John Day Company, New York, 1963.

Scientists think that the electric currents that produce the main field of the earth's magnetism are in the core. The spinning of the earth and the heat inside the core make the iron and nickel in the core move around. It is likely that these movements in the core produce the electric currents.

To make a map of the earth's magnetic field at the surface of the earth, scientists carry a compass needle from place to place and see which way it points at each place. Nature itself has made maps like these that show what

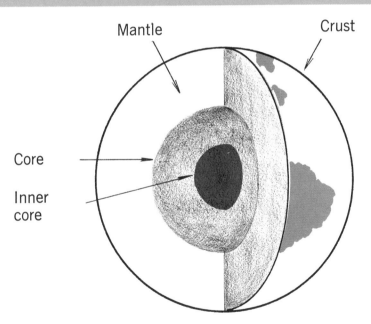

The earth with part of the outside cut away to show its inside layers.

the earth's magnetic field was like at different times in the past. These maps were made with little compass needles that are hidden in the rocks of the earth's crust. Many rocks in the earth's crust were formed from hot lava or melted rock that poured out of volcanoes. In the lava there were small grains of iron compounds such as magnetite, that are strongly magnetic. These grains were magnetized by the earth's magnetic field. Then each grain, behaving like a compass needle, lined up along the line of force. When the lava cooled and became solid rock, these grains were frozen into place, forming a map of the earth's magnetic field at the time that the rock was formed.

These magnetic maps hidden in the rocks show that the magnetic poles of the earth have not always been in the same place. They have wandered over the surface of the earth. The drawing on page 43 shows the path taken by the north magnetic pole during the last 800 million years. Starting in North America, it moved southwest across the Pacific Ocean, and then north across Japan and Siberia to where it is now. The wandering of the magnetic poles shows that the earth's mantle is probably slipping over the core.

The magnetic maps hidden in the rocks also show that sometimes each of the earth's magnetic poles has changed into the opposite kind of pole. This has happened on the

The heavy black line shows the path taken by the north magnetic pole as it wandered over the surface of the earth during the past 800 million years.

average once every million years.

The magnetic maps hidden in the rocks show, too, that Europe was once nearer to North America than it is now. They drifted apart about two thousand miles in the last 200 million years.

Magnetism of the Sun and Galaxy

The sun is a hot ball of gas that spins like a top. The heat has broken many of the atoms of the gas into charged particles. The motion of these charged particles produces magnetic fields on the sun. One field, the sun's *general field*, is like that of the earth, with lines of force joining a north magnetic pole to a south magnetic pole on the sun. The strength of this field at the surface of the sun is about one gauss. Other fields, about ten to a hundred times stronger, move across the surface of the sun in great storms. We see these storms as dark *spots* on the sun. These are called *local fields*.

There is a steady stream of charged particles moving away from the sun. The spinning of the sun makes the particles follow spiral paths, like water coming from a spinning lawn sprinkler. The particles pull with them the lines of force of the sun's general field and give them a spiral shape.

Sometimes a stormy part of the sun shoots a great fountain of gas into space. The fountain of gas pulls with it the lines of force of the local field. It stretches them like a rubber band into great loops, some of which reach past the earth. The loops form a magnetic bottle that traps charged particles that are inside it, but turns aside many particles that come from the outside.

The sun belongs to a great family of stars called the

Galaxy, or *Milky Way*. The Galaxy is shaped like a pinwheel, with spiral arms. It is also spinning like a pinwheel. Scientists have found that there are magnetic fields in these arms that keep the arms from breaking up. The lines of force of these fields run along the spirals in two sets. In one set, they point in the direction in which the Galaxy spins. In the other set they point in the opposite direction.

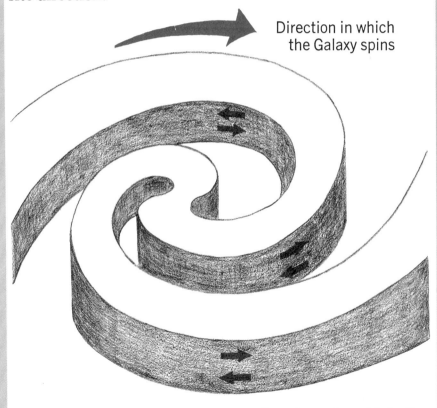

Direction in which the Galaxy spins

The small red arrows show the directions in which the magnetic lines of force in the arms of the Galaxy run.

Word List

Alnico (AL-nih-co) — A strongly magnetic mixture of aluminum, nickel, cobalt, copper and iron.

Antiparallel magnets — Bar magnets whose north poles point in opposite directions.

Bohr magneton (BAWR MAG-nuh-tahn) — The strength of the magnetism of a spinning electron.

Compass — A magnetic needle that points north by lining up with the earth's magnetic field.

Diamagnetic (DIE-uh-magnetic) — A thing is diamagnetic if it weakens a magnetic field into which it is placed.

Ferromagnetic — Strongly magnetic, like iron.

Gauss (GOUSE) — A unit of magnetic field strength, named after the mathematician C. F. Gauss.

Parallel magnets — Bar magnets whose north poles point in the same direction.

Paramagnetic (PAA-ruh-magnetic) — A thing is paramagnetic if it strengthens a magnetic field into which it is placed.

Pole — One of the two ends of a magnet where its magnetism is strongest.

Solenoid (SO-luh-noyd) — A wire wound into a coil, like a coiled spring.

Superconductor — A metal that has no electrical resistance.

Index

About the Authors

IRVING and RUTH ADLER have written more than sixty books about science and mathematics. Dr. Adler has been an instructor in mathematics at Columbia University and at Bennington College, and was formerly head of the mathematics department of a New York City high school. Mrs. Adler, who formerly taught mathematics, science and art in schools in the New York area, recently also taught at Bennington. In addition to working with her husband writing this book, she has joined with him on 24 other titles in the *Reason Why* series and drawn the illustrations for most of them as well as for many other books written by him.

Books by Irving Adler alone and books by him in collaboration with Ruth Adler have been printed in 83 different foreign editions, in 14 languages and in 10 reprint editions.

The Adlers now live in the country in the Town of Shaftsbury, near Bennington, Vermont.

PICTURE CREDITS

Pages 1, 12 and 39 — Bell Telephone Laboratories, Inc.
Page 21 — Brookhaven National Laboratory
Page 22 — Adapted from *Electricity and Wheels,*
      General Motors Corp.
Page 34 — After Verney and Helmann
Page 37 — MIT National Magnet Laboratory